There Is No Time Not to Live!

An Interview with Fran Grace about My Journey

Erin Lommen, ND

Edited by
Mary Bosch

There is No Time Not to Live!
© 2025 The Institute for Contemplative Life

All rights reserved. No part of this book, neither text nor images, may be reproduced or utilized in any form or by any means, electronic or mechanical, without explicit permission in writing from the publisher.

First published in the United States by The Institute for Contemplative Life dba Inner Pathway Publishing:

Inner Pathway Publishing
PO Box 1435,
Redlands, CA 92373
www.innerpathway.com

Cover photo of Erin and her dog, Jenga, courtesy of Jay Mead
Photo of Erin feeding the lion courtesy of Dawn Lommen
Additional photos by Erin Lommen

Publisher's Cataloguing-in Publication

Names: Lommen, Erin, author. | Grace, Fran, interviewer. | Bosch, Mary, editor.
Title: There is no time not to live! : an interview with Fran Grace about my journey / Erin Lommen, ND ; edited by Mary Bosch.
Description: Redlands, CA : Inner Pathway, [2025]
Identifiers: LCCN: 2025909682 | ISBN: 9781732318564 (print) | 9781732318557 (ebook)
Subjects: LCSH: Lommen, Erin--Interviews. | Cancer--Patients--Psychology. | Life--Psychological aspects. | Grief. | Self-actualization (Psychology) | Healing--Psychological aspects. | Suffering. | Meaning (Philosophy) | LCGFT: Self-help publications. | BISAC: BODY, MIND & SPIRIT / Inspiration & Personal Growth. | SELF-HELP / Death, Grief, Bereavement.
Classification: LCC: RC262 .L66 2025 | DDC: 616.9940019--dc23

Note: This book is not intended to be considered legal, medical, psychological, or any other professional service. The information provided is not a substitute for professional care. If you require or desire legal, medical, psychological, or other expert assistance, you should seek the services of a competent professional. The author, the publisher, and their employees, agents, and directors are not liable for any damages arising from or in connection with the use of or reliance on any information contained in this book.

Dedicated To:

*Jay, Brynn, and Dunal ~
with deepest love and gratitude*

and

*the Courage of the Human Spirit to say Yes to Life—
no matter what!*

Table of Contents

Foreword by Fran Grace..vii

Introduction: Letter from Erin to Fran..xi

Question #1: *Are there gifts from having this diagnosis?*.................1

Question #2: *What is unimportant in light of the diagnosis?*...........5

Question #3: *What is the meaning or purpose in your life right now?*.................9

Question #4: *What would you tell a person just diagnosed with cancer?*...........13

Question #5: *What has helped you the most in this journey to True Self?*.........17

Question #6: *What would you tell someone who is suicidal?*...........21

Question #7: *Could you write a letter to your children?*...................25

Question #8: *"Dark Night of the Soul"—what comes up?*................29

Question #9: *What was it like, getting sober?*................................33

Question #10: *How do you let go of shame, fear and anger?*...........39

Question #11: *What about grief?*..43

Question #12: *What has helped you deal with depression?*.............47

Question #13: *How do you cope with chronic pain?*......................53

Question #14: *How does it feel to be you right this moment?*.........59

Epilogue: Dear Reader..64

About the Author..65

About the Interviewer...66

About the Publisher..67

Foreword

I met Erin at a friend's house in 2023. We both felt that our meeting carried a purpose beyond itself.

At that time, someone close to me had just been diagnosed with late-stage cancer and placed on hospice. I was grieving with her, her spouse, and her young child. Even though I had recently finished training as a death doula, I felt overwhelmed by all the unexpected feelings that were coming up. I met Erin at the perfect time.

She had read *The Power of Love* book and felt a kinship with me; she could relate to my personal "story" woven throughout the book.

With determination, she pulled me aside at my friend's house and said, "For some reason, I think I'm supposed to tell you a few things about myself." She recounted a life-altering dream and told me about her terminal diagnosis.

She said, "I'm very selective about the people I tell about this diagnosis, because suddenly I go from being a person to being 'cancer.' It changes how they see me and relate to me. But I felt I was supposed to tell you."

I sensed the depth of Erin's journey. It occurred to me that we could support each other through a challenging time—I with my friend on hospice, and she with her inner journey. So, I asked her: "May I send you some questions about your life and also what it's like to live with terminal cancer?" Erin said yes.

And, so, for the next eighteen months, I sent questions to Erin, who answered them with rare authenticity. That "interview" is the basis of this book.

But, dear readers, please understand: We did not start out to make a book. Our dialogue began, simply, as a primal need to go deep into our suffering and extract the meaning out of it. My fourteen questions came from wanting to understand the experience of living with terminal cancer. How do you bear the suicidal moments? How do you fully live at the same time you're preparing to die? How do you deal with a diagnosis and not allow it to become the center of everything? How do you keep your heart open?

I saw Erin for the second (and final) time in 2024. She came to a four-day retreat, based on the book, *The Power of Love*. She was feeling pretty good with an unexpected remission from the cancer. Erin attended the retreat sessions with her whole heart, holding her well-worn book in her hand.

Alexander Vesely-Frankl was one of the retreat leaders. He is the grandson of Viktor Frankl, founder of Logotherapy and author of the famous Holocaust memoir *Man's Search for Meaning*. Logotherapy is "healing through meaning." Frankl's life and work comprise a vital section in *The Power of Love* book, so I wanted Alex to come be with us for the Retreat. He graciously traveled to California, all the way from Vienna, Austria, where he carries on his grandfather's legacy.

As Alex talked, I saw Erin's head nodding in vigorous agreement. She knew the truth of what he was saying from her own experience. Alex explained that meaning can be present, even in cases of inescapable suffering—incurable illness, Nazi concentration camps, murder of a loved one… Whatever the suffering that life brings us, and no matter what is taken from us, we still always have the freedom to choose our own attitude toward it.

Alex shared his grandfather's famous lines from *Man's Search for Meaning*:

> "… everything can be taken from a man but one thing: the last of the human freedoms—to choose one's attitude in any given set of circumstances, to choose one's own way."

Will we embrace what life is asking of us? Will we search for a meaning to life's difficulties? Will we say yes to life in midst of inescapable suffering, or will we constrict into bitterness and hatred?

"Life is your greatest teacher." This is the spiritual axiom we hear from the great mystics and sages. Spiritual teachers tell us to embrace everything that life is bringing us, for the very event that we might want to turn away from may very well be the means of our inner transformation—if we would only see it that way.

Alex quoted his grandfather, Viktor Frankl:

> When we are no longer able to change a situation, we are challenged to change ourselves.

And that is what Erin did. She said yes to life. She said yes to what her life was asking of her—even to the end.

The book you hold in your hands invites us to see Life itself as our greatest teacher. Erin shows us that even the pain of life will become our path of love and meaning if we are willing to see it that way.

I am deeply grateful for Erin's spirit and the love for Life that she expresses in this book. We finished it the week before she died.

—Fran Grace, Ph.D., May 2025

INTRODUCTION

Letter from Erin to Fran

This interview project is multidimensional and revealing for me. I have some different "selves" that often chime in and want a vote at the table, as it were. Then I ask to have my "senior editor" (my most integrated self!) to look and try to make sense of it. Sometimes I'm self-conscious and overly aware of you, my reader. Other times I am calm and clear with a desire to share something important to me—and maybe to you.

The truth is, I've spent most of my life wanting to hide, trying to be invisible. I worked to don an easy and benign public persona, one that is safe, nondescript, and free from criticism—a self that would offend no one, not draw too much attention, and allow me to slip invisibly through the world.

At one point, professionally, I became an educator and was called upon to speak publicly. Despite all my childhood habits of self-consciousness, introversion and fear, I found out that I felt a deep calling to communicate with audiences, and to connect people to what I considered vital and meaningful information. I enjoyed this dimension of my career. It was only the Covid pandemic that ultimately stopped its twenty-year momentum. When all the conferences shifted online, I couldn't find the energy and passion I had felt with live audiences.

Fran, the "story" you shared in *The Power of Love* book is daring. I was immediately drawn to learn more from you. Throughout your personal story, I heard courage, authenticity and clarity—I found it so real and often raw. This is our connective tissue I think—and so very essential to humanity in general. I wonder: Is humanity losing our way to raw authenticity? Everywhere I turn I see fake news and social media manipulations. When I come upon a person who is real, I feel that I have found a treasure.

Equally powerful was your experience with a true teacher. It held the magical combination of becoming deeply true to yourself and of finding a Guide who possessed Spiritual Truth! Your journey is inspiring and profound. I have heard and observed enough from you, Fran, that your trust and knowing that Dr. Hawkins was your teacher was clear and solid from the start. This teaches us all, I think.

I read this morning about Pema Chödrön's journey with her Buddhist teachers, in particular, her first teacher, Chögyam Trungpa Rinpoche. She spoke about how her inspiration and connection with him didn't happen all at once. Instead, Rinpoche needed to earn her trust. From the start, she found him cool and intimidating, and this made her doubt whether he was the right teacher for her. She knew she needed to experience him as a person in his humanness. This all occurred and allowed her to commit fully and completely to being his student. And regardless of the details, she was able to experience and trust his pure commitment in facilitating her (and all others) in "waking up."

I recognize that you are offering me the space and place here to unfold and reveal a true part of myself that's been in hiding. It is clear to me this morning that you are offering me this "teaching": a loving *bodhicitta* space for me to come further forward toward the Light and Awakening. I thank you for this treasured space, dear friend.

—Erin Lommen, April 2025

Question #1:
Are there gifts from having this diagnosis?

I am more open to changing and loving in places where I was closed before. I am more than ever dedicated to living deeply and with purpose.

Yet it might be the expected and usual response to say, "I have become so attentive and appreciative of life, grateful for everything, not taking anything for granted, traveling the World," and so on. But that is not so. It was especially not so at first. I was pretty much the same as I had been before the news, only now with a "terminal" cancer diagnosis. Finding my deeper purpose is a journey that continues today.

Initially, after learning this news, I was catapulted into a surreal mental and emotional fog. I waited for my Being to land, to find my footing, to be present in the here and now again. It took time. This dissociation was also a result of being triggered into a PTSD-like response. My mother died from this very same bone marrow cancer within four months of her diagnosis (in 2006). I knew what this disease could look like, and it scared me.

I felt deeply upset and very sad. So very, very sad. Trying to grasp that this life, in this body, would be coming to an end. I felt deep sorrow to imagine not being here anymore… not getting to see my beautiful children continue through life's stages to greater self-actualization, not growing older with my dear husband, not… the list goes on…

And I felt like who I was—was cracked open by the diagnosis. I found myself being changed. Like I had been a plant that had always leaned toward a particular Sun… and then that Sun evaporated— just disappeared. That Sun, the one I had always been drawn to…

that Sun from which I had drawn warmth, sustenance and meaning… that Sun that had been the source for my accomplishments, productivity, and future goals… that Sun was gone! It had always been the nurturer of my attachments, the momentum of my everything, the basis of my life… the driver of the forward motion.

But suddenly now, without expectations for the future, my earlier motivations fell off like leaves on an Autumn tree. And then mostly I felt empty. It all felt spare and barren. Because prior to this, everything that had ever held meaning for me seemed intertwined with a foundation of being here, being alive with a future of hope, planning, goals, and anticipation. I felt lost. It was a depressing free-fall for a while.

I quickly came to understand that the only Sun remaining for me, was the Sun that is the Source for Everything…the Divine Intelligence, the Universe, the Quantum Field, the Mystery. And my response was a deepening surrender and devotion to my spiritual path.

This newfound consciousness brought new challenges. These questions persisted for me: "How do I live in the here and now and be fully present and engaged in humanness, the struggles and the triumphs of our human condition… yet somehow still prepare to transition, to be done… to die? Should I even think about these things? Should I even try 'to prepare' for death? Or perhaps attempting to live fully right up to the finish line is the calling?" I'm still working on that.

Having this diagnosis does come with "gifts." But I might describe it, instead, as being strongly prompted (maybe even knocked really hard upside the head!) to grow into a consciousness I was not inclined toward without the diagnosis. And don't get me wrong—I wouldn't wish the diagnosis on anyone. But I do know it is my job here in this existence as a human, to work my butt off to accept what comes and do so with increasing compassion and purpose.

I have been allowed to grow and evolve with the opportunity of it. Like wow! I am here now, and I don't know how long I have left. What will I do with this time? What have I got to lose? What would be the best purpose for my efforts and attention? I feel braver! And I am softer in the face of getting hurt. I have a bittersweet sense of my life ending especially when I observe some others' beginnings. I smile big when I hear Louis Armstrong singing, *What a Wonderful World*, as I did today over lunch at a local restaurant.

Other "gifts": I do experience beauty and loving in relationships at a deeper level. It is all just so damn precious to me now. I am more generous with others in accepting and loving them, regardless. I don't want to be filled with petty judgment, but I am at times when it seeps in before I've chosen it. Nowadays, there's a more accessible kind of "refresh" button, and an easier path back to compassion.

Another bonus is I try to go for the truth—my truth—faster. I used to hang around people and situations that were not my Journey. I would find myself going with the flow. Now, I commit to developing relationships that I regard as authentic and I avoid superficial relationships, activities or socializing that requires a façade.

Besides having no cure, this diagnosis has many medicines and treatments, and this too is a kind of gift. When one protocol quits working, we have had another one to try. I have just received a new treatment. In 30 days, we will see one of three possibilities: Cure, Partial Cure, or No Response. To date, there has never been a cure for multiple myeloma. Could this be it?

Of course, I hope for Cure. What the hell. It will be very hard if there is No Response, but I might as well hang out in hope instead of despair while I wait.

So, the large "gift" with this terminal diagnosis as far as I can see today was to be granted a profound wake-up call and a belief that I must deal with my fear as best I can when it arises and then see what's left.

As a little girl, I used to shovel sand onto a framed screen and watch it sift through and leave all the bigger pieces, like shells and treasures from the lake. The bigger pieces (the meaning of life) that remain for me after filtering out all the sand and smaller debris are these:

+ Learning to Love with a wide-open heart—myself and others. Stretching to be more vulnerable than ever before and discovering that it's okay to risk and feel afraid while doing so. Loving "big" means valuing relationships and the well-being of others (my children, my husband, my siblings and family, my friends, everyone else, and all living creatures) above all else.

+ Deeper reverence and dedication to my Spiritual Path (meditation, spiritual reading, contemplation and devotion).

+ Insistence that I show up for Beauty (Art and Nature). These are my Soul's nourishment, reset button, and teacher.

Rock and water in the sunset.

Question #2:
What became unimportant in light of the diagnosis?

False self, that is, the layers of façade I developed to try to protect the innermost True Self.

Flowing with a current that is not my True journey suffocates my spirit. Yet so much of the time, as a young adult onward, I was trying to please others and be what seemed most acceptable, regardless of whether it felt authentic. I had spent decades unwittingly trapped by a compulsive need to be liked, to find acceptance, to be approved of and to avoid criticism.

In the past, I frequently accommodated others and tried to please in most social situations: home, friends, work. But my inner life was steering me steadily toward my True Self and I desperately needed this. So, the process of self-awareness and self-actualization didn't just start in 2017, with the diagnosis... it had been a long road since early adulthood. The pursuit of real contentment and the retrieval mission for my Wholeness was ongoing. It only became more urgent with diagnosis.

I felt I was mostly inept and unskilled at relationships and authentic connection with others, with its layered complexity, myriad complications, and confounding unpredictability. It was risky business, and I found myself too defended, hopelessly insecure, and mostly feeling lost, so I learned how to fake it.

An enduring commitment to this True Self Journey was deepened one night in 2012 with a life-altering dream. In the dream, I intentionally killed myself by jumping over the edge of the Grand Canyon. As soon as I'd jumped, I was filled with deep regret and inconsolable remorse. I had not meant to kill myself! I was free-falling past the steep canyon face, knowing that in seconds I would meet certain death. It was a life-altering wake-up call.

I awakened from the dream with wet cheeks and a stark awareness of its profound importance. I understood that my life needed radical change. It was the false self that I wanted to destroy. It was the false self that I was desperate to shed. It was the false self that was "killing" me. Yet "she" was practically all I knew of myself. Who was I without these decades-old layers of self that sought to accommodate and please at every turn? Who was I—the real me—underneath it all, when I was not trying so hard to be accepted by others?

With diagnosis in 2017, another urgency pressed on me. Life is short and living the way I had—had just revealed its limits. I had reached an end. Not knowing how long I had left… I understood that I needed to live authentically… to discover who I truly was. And I wanted to be loving toward myself, yet also honest and courageous for the inner work ahead.

Several unexpected changes occurred organically that sped up the journey to True Self. I transitioned out of private practice as a physician, and I stopped attending functions that had previously flattered me (to be invited, included) but held less meaning for me (required false self). I became even more committed to open-heartedness and vulnerability, first in my marriage and my relationships with my adult children, and then with others in my life. This also meant the loss of people with whom I had built relationship on unstable ground, namely the false self.

Another unexpected change was learning that I could ask for what I needed in relationships. I didn't even know that was a thing. I had always assumed that, in addition to avoiding conflict and criticism, I wanted what "they" wanted.

As a young girl, I had tried very hard not to need anything! So adult relationships were more like a complicated and seemingly unsolvable puzzle for me, rather than an intricate and dynamic dance. And I had not found the clues that pieced it all together until specific events like this diagnosis, the dream, and getting clean and sober "forced" me into it. I lacked a commitment to this process of uncovering my real thoughts and feelings—my truth—yet I hadn't even realized it.

Maybe this is simpler for others who don't experience threat and damage in their households in early life. Perhaps many people do not begin life as I did, with navigating it by forming a substantial layer of inauthentic self in order to insulate the True Self. But for some of us, that defensive layer is adopted because it's necessary to survival! In an alcoholic household like mine, hiding myself felt required. Healing trauma has allowed integration as a personality (that is, Big Self and little self consciously working "together")! I believe some of us are too clouded by the adaptive layers and defenses we learned in childhood, and continue through adulthood, to even begin to ponder purpose in a larger way.

My mother had a pure light quality. And her quiet yet steadfast devotion to her Spiritual path and unconditional Loving allowed her to emanate a brightness I have rarely witnessed. At the same time, her world often revolved around my dad (alcoholic and also dysfunctional with or without alcohol), and so she readily disappeared into her own version of hiding to survive. The alcoholic father and sometimes absent mother often left us (five children) to manage by our own devices. I learned how to survive, mainly by becoming important to others who would not throw me away. It was my childhood goal to have approval, and the best way to get it was to be accommodating and also to try to rescue my mother by bringing her Happiness.

The armor I wore 24/7 was thick and old, yet I had been lugging it around so long I didn't know myself without it. Diagnosis brought with it a sense of pressure, and feelings of urgency, to shed these last layers of defensive protection.

Question #3:
What is the meaning or purpose in your life right now? Why do you want to live?

I want to know more about my ability to show up as a substantial and purposeful self for any and all people and situations. I want to learn how to be more giving and forgiving in the face of my other selves who want to get more cozy and more comfortable. My terminal cancer diagnosis puts emphasis on this yearning and perhaps adds just a tinge of urgency! It is all prompting me forward in the search for True Self and awareness of ego-drivenness, and at the same time, divine generosity. We all have these, and I don't think we need to abolish the ego part or exaggerate the generosity part. We only need to discern what's what and then simply "be." Surrendering to this Truth is like a growing consciousness that supports us in an ever so gradual and oh-so-gentle process of quieting the ego and accentuating awareness.

To increase awareness and live in the Present moment. To evolve as a Human and as a Soul.

Getting my smaller "self" in alignment with my Higher Self has sometimes been a full-time job. Inner work, especially family-of-origin "work" for me, has been critical. This involves avoiding self-absorption or self-pity and obsessive rumination that's not constructive. Instead, clearing old layers away to reveal what's underneath is the work. But for my first few decades, despite being born with a very strong spiritual drive, I was often hijacked by inner turmoil, and this then created an outer life to match. This inner work was Job #1 for me.

When I relapsed with active myeloma in February 2023, I rapidly became ill, experienced bone fractures from the inside out (as is the course with multiple myeloma) and thought about the looming possibility of death. Thoughts jumped into my head of their own volition, like a cat darting across the road: What if I don't get into a trial? What if it doesn't work? Is this "it" for me? I felt afraid. I felt upset if it was about to end. It had taken me decades to learn how to live life fully, and now what if I was done?! I also felt a little curious.

Physical healing provides a daily sense of purpose and is central to my open-hearted journey of discovery to be Alive. Being sick with fatigue and increasing pain changes one's outlook, so that part of me (body self) sometimes wished it could end, or would End. Or at least this started to cross my mind. I was afraid to allow these thoughts and feelings too much as I wondered if they might direct the course of my illness and/or healing or at least contribute to it. As a doctor, I had spent decades in the rooms with patients and guided them in learning how to help the body heal with Love and Kindness directed toward the body self.

A connection between my body and my Higher Self emerged. I was aware of my bigger Self's knowing and trust that it was OK to ponder my death. I noticed a sense of peace in imagining transitioning to the Other Side. (Much of our Spiritual journey includes this knowing if we let it.) I continued to hear from my body self though, and she was experiencing fear and sorrow and unrest in becoming ill again so quickly. I wondered, How then was it going to go? What stood in the way of letting the disease just take me over?

One precious obstacle to resigning myself to dying during these moments was the Love I felt for everyone, and the Love they felt for me. This secret chord felt as if it would crack me open sometimes just from the sheer strength of it. LOVE. I felt lucky to have learned to love and to be loved so deeply in return.

So, it seemed that I had a choice to make: to give in or to try and save my life—this Life—this human self in a body. It is Love that gave me the will to fight—like glancing at my beautiful grown daughter as she prepared food for me. It sometimes takes a warrior's strength within to do everything possible to stay. It turns out that Love is this warrior's fuel, and it was a much stronger force than any giving up or giving in. I felt I had more purpose to fulfill, and it was not yet time to go.

I got into a medical trial (they take one patient per month at the University Hospital, a teaching hospital). Since getting enrolled, it has meant 180 doctor's appointments, lab-draws, procedures, and diagnostics in the prior six weeks. While I became increasingly ill, the demands of meeting all the requirements for such a trial at a teaching hospital, felt in and of itself, like it might be the death of me! And I wondered about others who did not have a clan to rally around them, to bathe them, cook for them, drive them, etc. I was, and am, very grateful for the love and support in my life.

The spiritual journey is not a straight line. I think for everyone, there are many detours and depressions, side trips and seductions (alcohol, nicotine, men, relationships, sugar, fear-based rumination, to name a few) along the way. By age nineteen, one addiction detour was completed, and I wound up in an inpatient facility for alcoholism. Stayed for three months. Then back out into the world and resumption of my Life's purpose and my Soul's quest.

In 1984, I was fortunate to hear my calling while on a solitary retreat at the nearby Trappist Abbey (which I sometimes visited to focus more deeply). I was called to be in Medicine. Natural Medicine. I finished up my pre-med coursework (BS) and began medical school (Naturopathic) in 1985. My purpose was to facilitate others in their Healing journey.

Is it ironic that my life's work and calling were intertwined with healing the body? I practiced Family Medicine for nearly forty years, and I loved every minute of it! And then when I received this diagnosis, I felt called away from my medical practice. It was as if the Universe said, "Okay, that was a pretty good run, but now it's time to do something else."

My sense of purpose hasn't changed, but I think how I am meant to express this purpose has changed. I left private practice as a family medicine doctor. In all the years of practice, I did not believe I would ever quit doing this. When you are fortunate enough to hear your Calling (your Purpose) and you say, "Yes," there is nothing like it in the world—because you are in alignment with something greater than yourself, the Universe, and you are helped along by It. I didn't think anything would ever change my deep desire to fulfill this Life's purpose—and then it changed; seemingly, with just a poof, it evaporated! With the terminal diagnosis, my identity transformed. I could no longer summon an ounce of what used to hold me in the rooms with patients, hour after hour, week after week, year after year. (It was dynamic, mysterious and sacred work, and I got to be its instrument.) Now it was clearly obvious that this era of being called as a physician was over, at least as I had known it. Perhaps I would need all my energy to focus on healing and being fully present to this cancer's journey.

PS: My thirty-day assessment after the treatment trial brought very good news. I am responding to the treatment and am nearly back in complete remission. I don't get to know for how long: three or six months? A year? A lifetime? No one knows. Yet the business of Living (not dying) is the loudest calling I can hear right now, and it must be done with purpose and consciousness…

That's it. That's all really. Every day we get to make a choice. Shall I open to my reason for living today or not? I say "Yes" today.

Erin feeding raw meat to lions at the Lion Habitat Ranch in Nevada

Question #4:
What would you tell a person just diagnosed with terminal cancer?

Well, shit.

"Begin with a broken heart" (Pema Chödrön).

This is a place of deep feeling. The seeds for compassion arise from this tender place, and you're going to need this "place" to inform where and how to go forward from here.

If we can get present with a bigger presence, a Self that can see the whole picture (wise witness within/inner observer), I believe we can walk through anything! We all have this Wise Inner Self, yet so often she is cluttered by day-to-day running thoughts and planning, etc. I suggest you let yourself feel the impact of this diagnosis—every cell of your being—only invite a part of you that can observe all of you to be present.

Try on the worst-case scenarios that are running amok inside you… these feelings, these thoughts, this damn diagnosis. There will be a voice running through your head that is scared—so, so afraid—the part in all of us that fears the worst when we hear the word "cancer." Your heart may feel broken for yourself. Give love to this part of yourself while it races around in your mind like a ball in a pinball machine bumping up against fear after fear. That voice is actually trying to help you find refuge but inadvertently gets trapped in an endless loop of fear-based rumination.

This is where the Wise Observer comes in. The diagnosis is a thing. Yes, a big thing. But still just a thing. *A diagnosis is not all of who you are, and it never will be.*

The part of you that is generating fearful thoughts and feelings is only one small part of you! It's not the entirety of who you are, even in this moment. There are other voices/other parts that are capable of other thoughts, new ideas, creative action. These other parts can observe the scared part of you, and at the same time remain in Wholeness.

I also suggest that you don't let the facts become you or own you.

Yesterday at a doctor's appointment, we discussed prognosis and outcomes for the newest treatment I've received. I do not like hearing these facts—the "data." It's just counter to how I am made—maybe how we're all made?—to talk about the likelihood of relapse. "Fifty percent get a year (or less) and then experience relapse, and the other half make it longer than a year."

We returned home from the doctor's office, and my husband seemed practically giddy with our new knowledge. The assessment showed that I had a "very good partial response" (not "complete remission" and not just "partial response"), so I should have at least another year to live! He found this news exhilarating. I was dissociating by then.

So, the old game of "If you had a year to live, what would you be doing? What would you do differently?" This is not a hypothetical exercise for me. I felt a little frozen at first. I am so very happy to feel well again. But I get stunned with such real data put in my face—like being tasered. It requires a disconnect for me to "chat" like this with a doctor. I think I do better with less information and instead a belief that anything IS possible… it just works better for me. And I feel more than a little concerned (a part of me experiences terror) about how this will go. I know we all need to live one day at a time—and to be in the moment as much as possible—but still…

Another thing: when physicians share data like, "You could have a year left, or you have stage four and your prognosis is such and such," what are we supposed to do with this? Is it truly helpful? Is this really part of medical advancement, to tell someone how long they are likely to live? Or would it be something else if oncologists said, instead: "There is every reason for you to believe you can be exceptional. Don't read about your diagnosis on the internet and don't listen to predictions and prognoses when others share stories. Protect yourself like you would from a poison. It's damaging to your Spirit."

When we receive a terminal diagnosis, I believe we must do whatever it takes to find our way back to our True Self (daily), and every day is different. Some days are hard as stone and some soft like a trickling brook. This True Self is naturally centered in basic goodness. We all have this at our core. So, while we engage ourselves fully by feeling our feelings and observing our thoughts, we can also enter this phase of life with a full and loving heart… and this may translate into helping to relieve the suffering of others.

Also, to receive a terminal diagnosis can be an incredibly powerful time, as we are capable of viewing "life" from an altered perspective. Sometimes this is positive and expansive, and sometimes it is small and suffocating—both of which are part of what it means to be fully human.

I am aware of how quickly the pathways in my brain become habitual roads I travel. Unwittingly, when we're diagnosed, we can carve out ruts of fear and isolation without even noticing. We may get into the habit of feeling certain ways. And in the case of terminal illness, it can be a downward spiral with feelings of hopelessness, sadness, anger, or loss. Conscious awareness is required in order not to get stuck in this mental and emotional descent.

I begin a day by becoming aware of how it feels to be "me" today. If it's a dark and heavy day, it will take more time and effort to get to ground zero. I gently welcome all the feelings that come with all that is my life, and with that Inner Observer present, I experience these feelings first, then move on to readings, meditation, and breakfast! I encourage playfulness! If I were not ill/living with this diagnosis, what would I do with today? Of course, much is not possible if we are so weakened and immobilized, but there might be a way to go toward our heart's desires by allowing others to help us.

Here are some examples:

+ I want to paint today. Friend, can you hold the brush and put it to paper? Yes there… and now this color… oh yes, and now going the other direction with the purple.
+ Please help me send a card to this person… I've been thinking about them…
+ I'd like to see sculptures by Rodin. Could you help me find a big picture book (the library) of his work?

- My heart feels broken today, would you mind putting on some Bach (my favorite music) and just sitting here with me?
- I want ice cream, Dairy Queen as a matter of fact! Could you bring me these different items: butterscotch dilly bar, lime freeze, marshmallow sundae, or just some soft serve in a cup? What do you love? Get those also! Let's have a sampling party and tell the stories they remind us of...

Aren't we all either in the process of living or in the process of dying? It seems possible to me that even while dying we're called to focus on living... whatever this looks like.

I'm going for a long walk in the woods with my pup now.

Question #5:
What has helped you the most in this journey to True Self?

There isn't one thing of course. And I think it must be shared, first, that it has almost always been hardship that brings me back to my truest self, and toward a True Self that's bigger than it was before the hardship.

So, to begin, what do I mean by True Self?

My True Self is my deepest and most purposeful and loving Self. There is a goodness that resides here. It is innately kind, warm, and giving. We all find this welcoming benevolent center in our innermost core when we get down to it.

And I have, as mentioned, an additional waking self that is quite easily distracted and derailed by humanness, muddled by negative thinking and critical impulses. This aspect of myself is ego-driven and can be consuming; I can spend whole hours lost in her, judging and forever evaluating self and others—"good or bad," "kind or mean," "better or worse," "attractive or ugly," "strong or weak," "peaceful or frenetic," on and on…

We are all so much more than a moment, and certainly we are better than the worst things we've ever done. I like remembering this. The human mind and the mud puddles that obscure our Truth are singularly protective and highly defensive, like a cocoon. Gotta smile at the irony here, don't we? Smile at how we're made: the very thing that allows us to survive and stay alive is the very same thing that suffocates our spirit and sometimes makes us feel like we're dying!

I think we each consciously have moments when we come to a place of sincere need/profound desire—an acknowledgment from within—this inherent longing to know ourselves more deeply. Like when I realized that my planned-on/planned-for career path was not what I wanted after all, and then I was left flapping in the wind for a time. Seeking authentic Self and direction was needed.

For me, seeking Self-direction is usually instigated by pain, confusion, or self-doubt. Many of my "aha" moments are like being slammed into the rocks. Yet, for others it could be a gentler, slower burn (like a niggling instead of a stabbing sensation). The pain of perceived rejection or betrayal has a particularly hot divination rod in this area of discerning our Truth. Small (ego) self is ever afraid of being cast out. We want to discover More… more about ourselves, more about how the world works, more about how relationships work in reflecting back to us our personhood.

Only with quiet am I ever able to hear the music I am meant to dance to. Paul McCartney once answered, when asked about the reason the Beatles broke up, that it was because they had grown so wildly popular and the crowds had become too huge. One night, while playing an outdoor concert to 55,000 people, he said, "We could not hear our own music!" This was the beginning of the end, he said. Only when I am moving to my own beat can I perceive Wisdom, Intuition, and Guidance. My touchstones for this are below.

Bringing Comfort
Recently, during one of my in-person discussions with a niece I am close to, she shared how, on one hand, the world's problems are so depressing and large that she feels it is too overwhelming and daunting to even try to do anything about it. She went on to say that she can feel so defeated and ineffectual, that it seems hopeless. She is twenty-seven years of age. However, next, she said something that has stayed with me: "So, I feel my job is just to try and comfort others." It's simply about showing up for each other, isn't it? This requires us to be fully present, so much so that I can see others who are suffering and be available to bring comfort to them.

Making Space
For this reason, I train in making space. Making space (quiet time, meditation, prayer) means no devices, no screens, no streaming, no

snacks, no sugar, no drugs, no self-medicating, no distractions. It may be quite difficult or even miserable to start building muscle for this! I wrestle with this from week to week. It's just part of being human! And the life I've chosen is an outwardly busy one with regular demands, frequent interruptions, and lots of noise.

No Social Media

In 2005, I decided not to participate in social media. This was not a noble gesture or grand discipline on my part. (Remember: I previously mentioned how I've been trying to hide my entire life). Nearly twenty years later, I am still clean and sober regarding social media. I am not suggesting everyone do this, or that it's even a good idea with today's possible connectivity and pace. Abstinence in this way doesn't fix despair, loneliness, anxiety, depression, and suicidal ideation, but I think it helps me refrain from getting caught up in distractions. It allows me to not get hooked by my insecurities or driven by my fears (whether I am liked or not liked). I am just saying that I chose this path because it suited me and was aligned with my commitment to learn how to be increasingly present in the here and now. Steering clear of social media helps me to keep my world smaller and quieter. Sometimes others ask, "Yeah, but how do you keep up with everything and everyone?" As it turns out, I keep up just fine. I hear within an hour or two what has happened in the news from others! And my family and friends text, call (yes some still use the phone function on a smartphone!), email, and write. I don't get to be the hermit I think I might have been in another life.

Today, I sit next to my daughter's hospital bed. I am showing up and hoping to provide comfort. I am committed to feeling my feelings about any and all of this, to stay current, and show up for and with her. She is experiencing post-Covid complications wreaking havoc with a previous autoimmune condition. This is day five, and she is having a rough time. No one is exactly clear—yet—how to stop the bleeding (literally and figuratively).

I am seeing, learning, that there is an opening, a gap in which to exist, between strong Nordic stoicism and emotional instability.

The path between those two extremes, in the middle, is awareness of what I am really feeling in this moment. Just showing up for her and for all of this and staying present with my vulnerable self allows me to be completely present here.

There is no other path for me but this "True Self" quest.

Despite being frequently pulled in multiple directions and the ever-present presence of the cacophony of existence, the minutiae of dailiness, we can continue to Seek. It can be exhausting and even the cause for soul-fatigue sometimes. Yet is there any choice— really? We are either busy living or we are busy shutting down and, well, dying.

Question #6:
What would you tell someone who is suicidal?

That I have felt this way too.

I don't know the details of what has brought you to this desperate place, but I do know that it is a dark and lonely place to find yourself in. So very dark. And I am sorry that you are suffering this way. It is a hell of its own.

Two times in my life I have pondered ending my life. The first was at fourteen years of age and the second a more serious pondering at twenty-three years of age.

At fourteen, I felt deeply despairing and profoundly alone. The straw which I found backbreaking at the time was the geographical move my family had just made. I left a small town with a population of 350 for a city of 60,000, and then I began high school. I was mentally and emotionally drowning. It crossed my mind during this time that I wished I were dead. I made no serious plans to end my life. And I ultimately shared this despair with my mother. I was not as alone with it anymore. She facilitated my climbing up and out of this dark place. It required her reaching for me, and me reaching back. And time helped too.

The second occurrence was when I was twenty-three years of age, and it was a more serious ideation. I had been clean and sober from alcoholism for three and a half years, and then I drank again and was not clean and sober anymore. Once I had slipped off the sober ledge, the alcoholism took me rapidly. Nothing mattered. I tried 12-Step meetings in the early mornings and yet found myself drinking by afternoon or evening. Soon I was shaky in the mornings, so I drank to steady myself in the mornings.

I had entered late-stage alcoholism in what seemed like the blink of an eye. I felt hopeless. What had helped me before no longer worked. I felt forsaken. I thought that alcoholism was ultimately going to kill me, so why wait? I thought I should just end it now!

The series of events that happened next were remarkable—perhaps even miraculous? Specifically, I decided I'd wait one more hour before jumping off a renowned bridge in my city (nicknamed "suicide bridge"). I drove up to the 12-Step meeting club where I had participated for three and a half years. I stayed in my car staring blankly at the place that had once meant so much to me and, in fact, had saved my life.

On this day, however, I remained in my car. I felt done with all of it. I was done trying. I just couldn't bring myself to get out of the car. I don't know how much time had passed as I sat in my parked car, but suddenly there was a man banging vehemently on the passenger-side window. I rolled down the window a bit, just enough to tell him, "Leave me alone." He said, "What are you doing sitting in there?" He was a homeless man whom we'd all seen at the Alano club from time to time, but I didn't know him and we had never attended the same meetings. I said, "I was just leaving." He said, "Naahh… C'mon into a meeting." I said, "No, they don't work for me anymore!" He said, "Is that so? Tell me about it."

I told him the short version through the crack of my car window—my past six months of drinking and rapid deterioration, and how nothing could help me now. He said "Okay, I get it. But I was wondering if you'd be willing to get out of your car and sit with me a bit?" I agreed. We then plopped down on the curb near my car and talked for three and a half hours. I remember little of what we spoke about, but I do recall my butt feeling sore from the hard cement. And I do remember going inside to an AA meeting following our curbside chat! And then I never saw this man again. That was over forty years ago, and I've been clean and sober ever since.

So, I ask you (the person feeling suicidal) to come sit with me on this proverbial curb for a bit. "Tell me, I mean really tell me, how it is you got to this place?" And I will listen intently. I will listen with all my might. I will listen while you exhaust all the words you can muster about how bad things turned out. I will listen while you blame this or that or claim there is no hope and never will be. I will listen until you are entirely emptied and out of words. I will listen until we are quiet. And I will listen in silence. Then I will ask, "Does your Truest, Deepest Self want to end this life, or is it another part of you? Tell me." And I will listen again.

I once read about a therapist who was working with an abused woman who repeatedly returned to "her" abusive man. Again and again, after each therapy session, she left the therapist's office with new resolve and conviction, strategies, and plans to get out and away from her abuser. She was trying to learn how to leave him, but each time she ultimately went back to this man. No amount of coaching, pleading, scolding, or cajoling was going to break this cycle. No planning, teaching, or counseling could penetrate deeply enough to alter her collision course with this violence against her personhood. The therapist had tried nearly everything, but he couldn't get through to his client. Through this experience the therapist finally learned to ask: "Is going back to him in alignment with your deepest values?" The therapist reported that she gave him a look he'd never seen before in any of their many sessions. The look held clarity. There was brightness in her pained eyes. She answered, "No, it is not." It was not in alignment with her True Self, and she knew it, even from the depths of her active PTSD. This changed everything. She began the work of breaking the cycle and was finally able to get out before it was too late! When we feel lost, finding our way back to our Deepest Self is the only path.

As for me, I have just learned (by getting online and looking at results from my blood draw yesterday) that I am relapsing. The cancer is on the move. Damn it. This diagnosis eventually figures out workarounds to the numerous types of treatments we've thrown at it. I am aware of the irony here—going from wanting to end my life forty-plus years ago, to now wanting to do whatever I can to save my life!

But I also get it when someone feels like ending their life. For a person whose despair exceeds their ability to cope and meaningfully process what is happening, suicide actually appears to be a solution. Faulty though its rationale may be, we are all capable of dipping into this deep dark suicidal ideation cellar. The trick is: What would it take for each of us to be willing to get out of the car and hunker down on the curb for a while? I did not know I was willing to do so that day, but I am forever indebted to the homeless man who insisted I sit with him on that curb.

What I believe to be true now is that I do not think pondering suicide means we're broken. (I know, I know… therapists worldwide would beg to differ.) No, I think it's finally an honest expression of how horrific we feel things have gotten. It's a sign that we do not possess the coping skills to manage all that's going on inside us anymore. It means we've tried everything mentally and emotionally that we know how to do, and it's not enough. We've reached a breaking point where we no longer know how to save our own lives, which is one of the deepest, most primitive instincts we all possess. It means we're ready for radical change but do not realize it yet. It means there is going to have to be an outside force that breaks the trance—my mother, the homeless man, someone we're willing to open up to (even if it's just a crack).

Compassion and Love saved me that desperate day over four decades ago. A stranger's awareness got me to the curb one last time and into a 12-Step meeting one last time. To say "Yes" to living. My mother also, by prying into my closed lonely existence, saved me. She extended her hand—and I grabbed it.

Am I aware enough—open enough, courageous enough—to pound on that car window uninvited? To insist? To impose upon someone to hold on a little bit longer? Am I willing to sit on a cold hard cement curb to witness my fellow human's despair (for three or four hours?) Can I show up in my Wholeness so someone else's broken spirit can come tumbling out and begin to mend? I want to.

Question #7:
Could you write a letter to your children?

LETTER ONE

To My Beautiful and Amazing Children,

I am writing today after a doctor's appointment. I've had a rough few weeks, physically and mentally. Relapsing is different this time around. The cells are not showing the secretory component like previously, so even though my IgA is low, I have developed a lytic lesion on the top of my sternum (manubrium), detected by me and confirmed by PET scan. (Bloodwork may not be as useful for detecting the status of the myeloma cells anymore.) My right hip, second left rib, and right posterior ileac crest have also been talking to me (pain). It has never been easy to have this diagnosis, but this recent relapse has been especially hard.

You two are the biggest and most central reason that I am fighting as hard as I can to stay here (be alive) and stay well (quality of life). Of course, I value life deeply for its own sake. You both have given me the most profound joy and deepest meaning I ever dreamed possible in this lifetime. So, I am forever grateful you chose me this time around, and I will do all I can to stay here.

I also get that this cancer journey is not just mine alone. I understand that you are both traveling an altered path as well, because of it... and all of us wishing it weren't so. But your fears, concerns and pain about this are not a small thing. Make room for it. And be extra kind to yourselves. This diagnosis and my ongoing battle play in the background of your days too, I realize.

I want to open up the channels to share and talk freely about this. I want you to tell me what works best for you. I want to share honestly and help you process your thoughts and fears if I can.

Can we talk about dying? Of course. I invite you to do so openly. I am not going anywhere right now. There are still more options for me to treat and return to remission, but a time may come when solutions are limited… and I don't want to wait until then to go deep with this. Believe it or not, there are gifts to be had from sharing and growing together through so serious a thing.

I never would have known how fierce and brave I could be if it were not for you. Once I had you, I grew into knowing that there wasn't anything I wouldn't do to care for you, to protect you, to love you the best way possible!

Do you think I do all this self-help stuff for fun?! I have intended to clear and clean out all the channels you have to me (my inner work), so that what I offered to you would never diminish you in any way, but rather, would make you better and stronger.

I do wish I had shown you more of my vulnerability when we were navigating choppy waters through your childhood. I didn't know how to show you my vulnerability at that time. I thought that being strong was the best way to help you grow strongest. Now I know that if I'd shown you more moments when my heart was breaking, you would have witnessed true strength, and you would solidly understand that you could have your heart broken and still be okay. More than okay! In this way you could have seen my resilience and recognized that you have this capability too.

Having your heart break is quite beautiful, actually, because it means that you have experienced intense Love and profound Care. It's a positive thing to feel such Loss. I hope your hearts have been broken a few times already and that you will have several more heartbreaks in your lifetime. Regarding Love, I want you to Care wholeheartedly and Risk with all your might. I want you to experience, like I have, how much bigger your Being becomes and how much more tender you grow with each such heartbreak. It is a really good and rich life to Love so completely, to care so surely, and to know with certainty that Love IS what it's all about!

Thank you for loving me back so soundly and so fiercely. Your life partners and your close friends will consider themselves lucky to experience the steadfastly loyal and deeply pure version of Love you bring to the table. You must know, I consider myself extremely lucky to have shared this life with you. I love you.

Sunset over hills.

Question #8:
What comes to mind when you hear the phrase, "Dark Night of the Soul"?

It's where the spiritual rubber meets the road!

Am I still walking through this darkness? Or have I come through it? It has been a long while since my soul returned to me cleansed and rejuvenated, and I am trying to be prepared if this is where I will live now. Is this a new normal? It is so dark in these moments where there is nothing bright, no saving Grace to ponder about this kind of empty suffering.

This time, it began through the holidays, or actually in early December. I could feel my hope and my buoyancy leaving. The thoughts of dying came more often; no, it was not like I was wishing it, but rather, it was the natural outcome of my health deteriorating so rapidly (myeloma relapse).

During all this, I signed up for the next treatment as fast as I could. I have surrendered at a deeper level. I am willing to walk this path, yet on this Friday morning when it's all still new since leaving the hospital, I feel immense loss and pervasive weariness. My hands and feet feel scorched as if the skin has been burnt, my mouth raw and numb with 100% loss of taste. There are more side effects. The soles of my feet and my palms are peeling layer by layer each day, and I have to wear gloves nearly 24/7 as my fingers are too raw for the regular environment. Fuck! I want to apologize to my sweet body for putting her through so, so much! I am sick of everything this morning. I say to my body, "I am sorry, my beautiful container! You are so fierce and tenacious! Should I stop putting us through this?" An Inner Sense-like Guidance, Wisdom, and Intuition, all in one, felt as if it were still holding me tight, in a remote way during this dark time, and it answered clearly: "No. If you are willing, then let's stay! There is more to fulfill."

So, back to the "dark night of the soul": I feel alone and forsaken during this. I feel depressed and sour about most things I think about at these moments. I don't really even want to talk with others at such times. I have cultivated so many beautifully rich relationships/friendships, but that whole and often vibrant woman I can be appears to have left the premises.

When I tune in to a meditative frequency during this time, it feels nearly turned off, like there is nothing, no one, no higher frequency. I am going to keep walking forward, one wobbly weak step at a time. I am going to allow myself to feel how dark it is in this place. I'm not going to pretend it is better or different than it is; I am going to just be.

While I was in the hospital for those ten days, I lost my enthusiasm, and my spirit felt broken. I felt traumatized by it all while there. Mostly I was so altered by the steroids that I felt crazed and unstable. I was practically begging them to lower the dose as I was so uncomfortable, but my pleas fell on deaf ears and I was in a fight-or-flight terror response for three to four days straight, without sleep. It was kind of like being indoctrinated into a cult. In the end, there was resignation, and they won. I got the shots, took the pills, and succumbed to every request. I wanted out, but I feared I wouldn't get released as soon if I tried to champion myself in any way.

This was two weeks ago. I am slowly recovering from the past ten weeks. I can now reflect that it's as if the medicines and the physical body itself put a veil over True Self at these times, because I could not feel my center, my sense of Self. Is this a spiritual gift disguised in cancer's clothing? I mean, after all, we are always talking about shedding the ego-identified self.

I think not. No. I would say it's not the same. Cancer is not a gift in that way. In the other scenario, with spiritual work, the ego-free state comes with the Consciousness that one is intentionally letting go of ego identity. Rather, what I'm describing with illness was more like a loss of presence, like a removal of the Being from mindfulness and the day-to-day experience of a remoteness... being not all here, like a no man's land... and it's a spiritually devoid place. I have felt tossed about by spiritual angst and profound emptiness a few times in this lifetime.

The darkness arrives unbidden and does not announce its length of stay. Of course, every time it seems like it might never leave. I have learned to try to surrender to it, with it, even though there are parts in me screaming, "No, no! Don't succumb!" I fear it could consume me!

I think of Mother Teresa and her own wrestling with emptiness and longing for spiritual connection, like a continual Dark Night of the Soul, for decades. My heart breaks for her if this is really how it was for her. We can't really know what her deepest inner struggles were about, yet to learn of her questioning and longing is enough to know that she visited this dark place often. I also think of the story of Christ on the cross, and those very dark and alone moments: "Why hast Thou forsaken me?"

And then very recently, while I was in hospital, my sister and I shared a "Dark Night," though we were not together. She spent a night in jail (her first time to be jailed for drunk driving), and I thought how devastatingly lonely it must have been for her to gradually become sober and find herself with seven other women, sitting on a hard cement slab in a cell.

My sister had come to town to be with me, to support and help me while I was hospitalized, but her addiction had other plans for her. This is an entirely different story and not for this discussion, but anyone who has lived with, or loved, an actively addicted person knows the heart-breaking predictability with which the addict will defy, disappoint, and demolish rational planning, good choices, and reliability. I felt heartbroken when I imagined her there in that jail cell. She must have had a very Dark Night. And it was also an added dimension to this Dark Night of the Soul feeling for me as I waited to hear what had happened to her. Why had she not shown up to the hospital? Was she okay? Where was she?

Pema Chödrön, the Buddhist teacher, says we have to train in experiencing groundlessness (and surrendering to uncertainty) first in order to prepare for big events when it can feel like our world is collapsing. And second, in general, because the solid ground we cling to is not Real and will be forever changing.

I believe we are supposed to know and experience this aloneness, this emptiness, these "Dark Nights" as individual humans. We have to glimpse it or dwell in it for a time in order to be forged and shaped as Spiritual Beings. It is inherent in inhabiting a body and walking the face of the Earth. It's like fitting into our skin more fully. To completely inhabit this life, we have to dare to plunge into its psychic and sometimes tragic depths, as well as soar on its spacious and beautiful skies. There is no other way to know this life's dimensions.

Like anyone, I don't know how long my life will last, how long I will be in this body, this lifetime. I do know that with a terminal diagnosis, Life is brought into razor-sharp focus at times of relapse, that it might be sooner rather than later. I do wish, at times, this did not happen. It's a roller coaster ride. And I also continue to find acceptance on the other side of this feeling of despair and regret. It IS okay. I will continue to dedicate myself to deepening my spiritual awareness and to align my behavior with this Consciousness. And then try to show up and accept the world just as it is.

Question #9:
What was it like, getting sober at a young age?

What would you share with young people (in their twenties and thirties) who want to be free from alcohol, drugs, and other compulsions? And what about that fear of missing out on life if they sober up at a young age?

> Between stimulus and response there is a space. In that space is our power to choose our response. In our response lies our growth and freedom.
> —Viktor Frankl

First a story about losing the power to choose.

I filled the large clawfoot tub (my apartment building was over one hundred years old) with the hottest water the tap could muster. Then with steam rising off the water's surface and fogging the medicine cabinet mirror that hung above the nearby pedestal sink, I padded back to the kitchen in slippers and robe to grab the half-gallon carton of vanilla Swiss almond ice cream out of the freezer. And I remembered also to grab a strong spoon. (My freezer froze desserts so solidly that this dessert could bend a spoon better than Uri Geller back in his heyday!) I hurried back to the tub. I slid into the hot water holding the ice cream container above the water, as if protecting a precious and rare first-edition book. In the comfort of the heated water, I then tasted the wonderfully creamy vanilla and savored the crunch of the dark-chocolate-covered almonds. In this moment I cared less about everything and everybody. I was experiencing glee for this delectable and full container of ice cream.

As time passed, and the water cooled, I kept running more hot water into the bath. And spoonful after sturdy spoonful, the pleasure of extreme indulgence was mine. Later, I dropped the empty container on the floor outside the tub and lay back in the now-tepid water. Yes, I said "empty" container. I was dazed. I was fatigued. I was altered. I had never consumed this quantity of ice cream in a single sitting in my life!

I thought, *How pathetic you are. This is no worse than drinking.* I was a twenty-three-year-old recovering alcoholic with three and a half years of continuous sobriety. But now, with this quantity of sugar under my proverbial belt (and in my brain), my next thought shot through like lightning across the sky: *You might as well drink!*

Next, without hesitation, I got out of the bathtub, dried myself carelessly, quickly dressed and rode the rickety elevator with the accordion iron gate (the oldest one in the city of Portland) down to the ground floor from my 12th-floor apartment, and I hurried out of my building. I could feel the tips of my hair damp and cold in the November air. I practically ran to the nearest convenience store on the corner of my block, a Plaid Pantry. I bought a six-pack of beer and thought, *I will find some hard liquor while I drink this.*

And poof! Just like that, three and a half years of continuous sobriety were gone. There I was, a "recovering" alcoholic, and a compulsive sugar binger, alone with my dual intoxication at the corner of 11th and Clay, looking for a liquor store.

First, I was twenty, then twenty-three years of age, when I became sober from drugs and alcohol. I was frustrated and sometimes angry about finding myself in treatment places, and then in AA rooms, mainly filled with old men! I frequently felt isolated. I often felt insecure and wondered if I could ever have a good life. I had often thought I was way too young for this! Sobriety at age twenty-three, was I crazy? I'd barely gotten out there and tasted life! People my age were socializing, partying it up, and having a blast (I imagined) with alcohol and recreational drugs. Why should I have to quit so young?

Yet, three years earlier, at twenty years of age, I'd already bottomed out. College wasn't working, relationships weren't working, life wasn't working. At age twenty, I'd gotten help. And I worked hard in the programs that were offered to me. I joined aftercare outpatient treatment for a year and a half, after my twelve weeks of inpatient treatment. I attended AA meetings, got a sponsor, and worked the 12 Steps.

After three and a half years clean and sober, I took that fateful bath described above—and went back out drinking again. I was unhappy. I did not find joy or peace in this "new," sober life I had created. I was convinced that the "old" life of drinking and partying had to be better out there, and that I was missing out on too much. I wanted to join the excitement and the adventure.

But here's the thing: "Adventure" is not what met me at my welcome-back-to-drinking party! Rather, this "gala" opened up a very deep and dark pit into which I promptly fell. I was alone. So, so alone. There were no gregarious gatherings, no fun moments with friends, no loud laughter. I felt profound despair and inconsolable hopelessness. And I could only reach for more numbing elixir when the suffering became unbearable, which it did—daily.

There is good news and there is bad news. The good news is that we have two substantial centers in our brains that are amazingly efficient and adept at the functions they perform and at helping us navigate the twists and turns in life. The bad news is that they are not on speaking terms!

Once we are in the throes of compulsions and addiction, we are no longer in charge. That train left the station, and the conductor of this locomotive is not us, or at least not as we know ourselves to be. We lose the ability to be in charge of our choices as time and addictive behavior progress. It can be said that we have two minds: the pre-frontal cortex and the amygdala/limbic system. But these two distinct areas do not communicate with each other.

The area of the brain that is our executive function center—pre-frontal cortex (language center, decision-making center, goal-setting center, rational thinking center, impulse-control center, the give-a-shit-center!)—is shutting down and even atrophying when we are in the throes of addiction. And then it's just a limbic system/amygdala free-for-all. This is the primitive brain (the fight-or-flight-or-freeze center, the feel-good center, the impulsive throw-caution-to-the-wind center). To an observer, it is crazy to watch an addicted person's behavior because it is often very erratic and irrational.

Compulsions are just like substance addictions. The dopamine pathways drive behavior in order to try to get more of the feel-good chemicals. It can be shopping, cleaning, internet, sex, internet sex, gambling, video games, relationships, overeating or not eating, and so on. As evidenced by the myriad 12-Step programs (over fifty to date, from Emotions Anonymous to Debtors Anonymous, etc.) and self-help groups, many behaviors become compulsive and addictive. And addiction leads us down an empty hallway that is destructive, demoralizing, and deadening.

So, there I was, experiencing my compulsive overeating, which cascaded into my alcohol addiction, which then spiraled into my depression, which finally plummeted into wanting to end my life. I could not see any way out. I had tried everything I knew to stop the bleeding, but to no avail. After four miserable months of spiraling down, I only wanted it all to end.

Let's face it: Escaping is the goal when we reach for a compulsive fix. We feel afraid: Am I enough? Will I be successful? Am I lovable? We judge ourselves harshly and imagine everyone else out there to be doing well, not suffering with any of these feelings. Then we find a behavior or something we can consume that helps us forget about all this. It makes us feel good for a minute or three! To get away from our present state, we use whatever works and is available. Distraction is at an all-time high. Screens lend themselves to never having to be alone with ourselves, our thoughts, our feelings. We're trying to outrun the pain and anxiety we are experiencing. And in today's culture, we definitely don't learn how to show up or stay.

The way home to healing and sanity and freedom varies for each of us. But what is true for all of us is that willpower doesn't work to help us stop, control, or stem the tide with addiction and compulsive behaviors. That's because these two parts of our brains are not on speaking terms. While one (prefrontal cortex) is shrinking in its capacity to steer our lives, the other (limbic/amygdala) is growing in its dominance. On Monday morning, we can swear to ourselves we will never take another drink, or never binge on sugar like that again, but by that evening (or maybe we make it until Wednesday afternoon), we then suddenly find ourselves gripping two hot fudge sundaes or a double shot of vodka.

The brain cannot change itself and cannot help us get back on track when in the throes of compulsions and addictions. It will drive us to the death, seeking "more." And keep in mind, some of us are built differently from others. We have "it"—a genetic propensity for addiction. We may get an uber dose of a dopamine surge from shopping online or playing poker or having a drink. While we all like to feel good, some of us glimpse euphoria!

The more we practice our addictions and compulsions the more ingrained they become. And now a paradox: The only way back appears to be through surrender. We know this to be true for spiritual growth. We do not evolve if we are only ego-driven and working to control life around us. The same is true for compulsions and addictions. The old adage is true: "We have to want help." Yes, we have to hit a desperately weary place. We have to give up and surrender. We must seek change and help during this desperate time. And we have to be prepared for when the amygdala/limbic system fires back up and tells us it really wasn't so bad—hence the groups, the fellowships, the congregations to lean on in those weakened self-deluded moments.

Respecting the body's neural chemistry is essential. It's real. You may not have consciously bought the ticket to ride the compulsive/addictive roller coaster you find yourself on. But once you're on it, surrender is the only stop lever available. As corny as 12-Step groups may seem to some of you, they truly work, as do other programs for healing. Making peace with the human race must happen. We need to learn to trust and love others—and ask for help.

That's what credible solutions do. They help us learn skills for how to meet our needs. We are not alone, yet compulsive behaviors isolate us. It's our secret. We each must return to our human village to learn to live well and experience our Wholeness.

For me, Life has continued to grow into a rich and deeply satisfying mosaic as I heal and recover. This has been over a period of decades (age twenty-three to present). I have nurtured a True Self that quickly outgrew my false self. I learned how to meet my needs. I learned how to manage stress. I learned how to unravel my relationship addiction and instead invest in more satisfying functional relationships with individuals who can love me back. And I learned how not to have half a gallon of vanilla Swiss almond ice cream in my freezer (maple nut, however, is safe with me)!

Question #10:
How do you let go of shame, fear and anger?

How do you apply Dr. Hawkins's "letting go" method to everyday life, attachments to people, getting free of shame, fear, and anger? (Dr. David Hawkins has written many books as a physician, researcher, and spiritual teacher, including *Letting Go: The Pathway of Surrender*, which you studied deeply.)

Dr. Hawkins's *Letting Go* elucidates Universal Truths, and we all possess this knowing deep within. Yet how to access this Wisdom and Intuition day-to-day is the trick! *Letting Go* changed a basic principle for me, having to do with identifying how I am feeling—and then feeling it! Reading and studying *Letting Go* gave me tools for how to increase my awareness of my current mindset. For example, am I experiencing love for my fellow humans or am I slinking down into the murky shallows of judgmental separation? Both are dimensions of humanness. And Dr. Hawkins brings detailed guidance for how to climb the consciousness ladder, up and out of negative emotional states.

Feeling feelings when they occur are foundations for emotional health. This natural process is the basic ingredient in the recipe for the freedom to be true to ourselves and to experience deep well-being and happiness. When we are avoiding feelings, oddly, we stay stuck in the residue of the feeling.

If I say "that hurt" to someone whom I feel affronted by, it has very different consequences from not saying anything at all, and instead thinking to myself: "What an ass, you are so self-centered. I can't believe you would say that to me. I'm not going trust you anymore. You do not deserve my kindness." Next, I may then feel justified in growing a resentment, and I might also start to feel superior to this person, as if I'm the "good" person and they're the "bad" one. The irony is that, when this occurs, I am doing to them (in my mind) the very thing I am judging and criticizing them for having done to me!

Feeling feelings sounds simple, but it isn't easy if you're like me and you learned early in life how not to feel feelings. I didn't realize for decades that I was "thinking my feelings." I could name them, brood about them, create resentments about them, craft storylines surrounding them, but I did not actually know how to feel them. The *Letting Go* book emphasizes the innate thing that happens when we feel the feeling in the moment: the emotion dissipates. Poof! Just like that, it just passes on through. The brain scientist, Dr. Jill Bolte-Taylor, says that an emotion's lifespan is ninety seconds (in her book, *My Stroke of Insight*.)

With shame, fear, and anger, I find that the negative consequences of feelings occur from my knee jerk reaction to get away from them. It's my resistance to feelings that causes the suffering, not the feelings themselves. The escaping, the running from, the diversion tactics—these are what destroy the quality of our lives, not the actual feelings!

Letting Go illuminates this truth poignantly. We create and believe in the storylines that our emotions elicit, and this constant internal monologue, which plays incessantly, causes so much trouble! Dr Hawkins calls it "the endless intellectualization and elaboration." We will play the same stories again and again in our minds, like a looping one-song wonder, and this quickly grows neural pathways and becomes part of "us." When we remember this or that feeling, we play that same song again and again, not unlike a scratch on an old vinyl record. I call it "death by rumination" because it strangles the vitality out of us.

"Shame." I am not surprised that this state of consciousness is at the bottom of the list on Dr. Hawkins's consciousness map. I *am* surprised that I could experience this state for decades and manage as well as I did!

Shame was not a concept that had been very developed or discussed in everyday chats or pop psychology when I was in my twenties and thirties. But I do recall very clearly the moment my eyes were opened to it. I was thirty-three years old. I was the mother of a five-year-old and a three- year-old, and parenting had brought forward layers of undealt with, unconscious, issues (buried and unfelt feelings) and behavior patterns (of my parents) that I was repeating. Yes, I was repeating their mistakes, which I had sworn I would never do!

I was in a dentist's office for my appointment. A magazine, *Atlantic Monthly*, caught my eye with the front cover caption: "Shame." I promptly grabbed it and sat down to read about a condition I had been experiencing all my life but had never heard it named: Shame! It was a tremendous relief to hear this psychologist/author speak about it with such clarity and warmth.

I had always felt less than everyone. I felt worthless and afraid to show anyone who I really was because I was filled with self-loathing and self-contempt. As I began to read about this, as a learned condition with the faulty beliefs accompanying it, I wanted to weep. We can be "shamed" as young children and as a result learn to perceive ourselves as defective. Here I was, reading an article in the dentist's office, where most people in the waiting room next to me were nervously awaiting oral drilling and scraping, and I had just been made privy to a life-altering revelation: There had never been anything wrong with me—I was not defective after all!

Fear and anger are interesting, in contrast to shame, because I do not think these two emotions are learned or acquired feeling states. I think these two emotional states are there from the start and are integral to our survival. The fight-or-flight response is basic to our nature. It's how we are built. And as emotions that are elicited in day-to-day life, these two emotional states of fear and anger would be benign, if we just learned how to feel them. But by repressing or suppressing them, we remain stuck at lower vibrational levels.

A trusted friend and I studied Dr. Hawkins's *Letting Go* very deeply, two times, and this changed things for me. It gave me a springboard from which to rise. Living mostly in negative vibrational states is miserable. *Letting Go* taught me the how and why of feeling feelings. It has been my self-help manual for restoring emotional freedom and raising self-esteem.

And I haven't even begun to explore how beautiful existence can be when we rise to higher vibrational levels! We get to choose. But it's as if we develop a belief in our negative emotional states, as if they are the reality, and then we attach to them and fortify them with storylines. Our ego gets the payoffs in this cycle, and we never look back (or up!). This generates a perspective rife with more fear and more anger. A significant liability with these two feelings is that they readily transform into extremes if they are not felt and released: terror and rage. Terror and rage are often the cornerstones upon which Complex PTSD and depression are built.

Feeling our feelings requires vulnerability. That is the work! It includes learning how to be gentle and kind yet painstakingly honest with ourselves. How to be vulnerable again? It is a worthy journey back, but I have found it challenging too. We don emotional armor with solid reasons as children. Shedding this thick and clunky armor, this façade, requires tenacious commitment and substantial effort.

I figure that we who have been catapulted out of negative emotional states of existence are the lucky ones. Getting cracked wide open (emotionally) is not fun. Life events and emotional catastrophes will be visited upon us all. Awakening to a higher consciousness can be the buried gold we've been seeking and can be the hidden treasure in the rubble of our pain and sorrow. And we get to choose. There will be many crossroads in a lifetime. We will be devastated by numerous events. Will we resist and hang on for dear life as we've always known it, or will we let go and allow the transformation? We get to choose.

Question #11:
What about grief?

How has *Letting Go* impacted the way you are walking through your current challenges?

Experiencing my own unwanted feelings is key to feeling free and remaining true to myself. *Letting Go* held my hand as I learned how to do this. Grief is so important to our dimensional human experience, yet so easily suppressed and avoided.

An interviewer once asked the 14th Dalai Lama if he had any regrets, and he answered, "Yes." He then shared that he felt responsible for an elderly monk's death. He shared the story about this monk who had come to him for guidance in a highly advanced and complex Buddhist practice. The Dalai Lama understood how many years were required to train in this practice, so he explained to the older monk that there were other practices that better suited his age and status at the monastery. The next morning the Dalai Lama learned of the monk's death, and a suicide note: The monk had taken his life so he could begin his next lifetime as a younger monk and learn this practice. The interviewer then asked the Dalai Lama, "How did you get rid of the grief and regret?" He answered, "I didn't get rid of it; it's still there."

Grief. When we learn to feel our feelings as they arise, as Dr. Hawkins describes in *Letting Go*, we are free to experience the present. I'm not certain we ever "finish" with grief. Rather, perhaps we learn how to make room in our hearts for the ache of the loss and we learn how to actually grieve, that is, feel the feelings and not just think about the sadness or empty longing.

In *Letting Go*, Dr. Hawkins speaks of vibrational levels, and where much of the human race hangs out is not at the states of "Peace" or

"Love"! "Grief" is a state that hovers near the bottom of his consciousness map, and I think it's a common quicksand that's easy for any of us to sink into if we stay stuck in grieving.

Over seven years ago, I was diagnosed with a cancer that has "no cure" (multiple myeloma). Initially, I felt pummeled by this news. The knockout punch had been thrown and landed squarely. I felt laid out, totally flattened by it. Attachment to living is oh so strong! For me, by then, however, there was nowhere to go but to stay with my experience, to surrender to the impact of this news, to deeply feel the fear and the sadness and the grief of it.

Depending upon where I am at, I find that I must walk through each day, experience some symptoms, engage each new treatment, stumble for a while with each relapse, experience renewed hope with each remission, and learn how to live with the unknown in a very immediate way. I have a few very sad, low, and blue days. I don't get to know if a treatment will work or not, and I don't get to know each time I relapse if I'll get to return to "living well" again. If I choose a treatment, there is no guarantee it will help me live a bit longer. We always say, "live each day to the fullest," because we never know when something could happen and it's our last day.

The grief of perceived loss—loss of my life, my attachments, "me"—is a new companion that I've had to learn how to live with. I find that feelings of sadness and loss also bring up other feelings of sadness and loss, so perhaps I have a backlog of unexpressed grief? Or maybe this is the nature of grief—like there's a place in our hearts where we feel the painful ache of loss and then, when we lose someone or something again, we feel it, along with acknowledging that this heart-breaking graveyard is also filled with the bones of other past losses. We may have to feel those older, buried feelings again, too, upon entering this "cemetery."

I was grieving the loss of my mother for many years following her death. My attachment was full-bodied and partly unconscious. She died eighteen years ago. Her death was my deepest introduction to gut-wrenching grief. Even though we knew we were losing her, I could not prepare for it, try as I might. It was only after she was gone that I could allow myself to experience the crushing anguish and profound sense of desolation and loss. Dr. Hawkins addresses grief by explaining that it's helpful to identify which part of us is hurting (child, parent, or adult). In this case, my child was activated and experiencing an overwhelming sense of abandonment and loss.

Forty percent of U.S. adults will get cancer. There are 18 million people living with it right now. So, the reality is that I am not the only one! The trap for any of us is to feel unique in our suffering, which can result from any aspect of life. I work to stay in alignment with my Higher Self and not slip off into ruminating and storylines. Self-pity is a toxic state of being. Self-pity breeds the erosion of our agency and empowerment, and it lands us in victimhood. It's like being dead in the water, where it's quite easy to sink.

What have I got to lose—what do any of us truly have to lose, getting free of fear and ego, learning to love ourselves and others—no matter the flops, the failures, and faux pas?! I love the freedom I'm growing into. Of course, I wish I'd had more of this in my early adulthood! And yet, I can only feel grateful for the wonder of growing into it now.

Developing an astute ear for the voice of the True Self, and then following its lead will never misguide us. Through Dr. Hawkins's book, we learn to feel the grief of loss. Life is filled with loss. We won't escape it. And maybe, just maybe, we can find freedom and meaning in it. I think it may all come down to really feeling the loss and then letting it go. If we don't allow our grief to be felt and experienced, then it isn't possible to ever let it go.

Question #12:
What has helped you deal with depression?

What has helped you personally deal with depression—emotionally and spiritually? As a naturopathic physician, what have you observed as being helpful to others in dealing with depression?

> "I felt very still and empty, the way the eye of a tornado must feel, moving dully along in the middle of the surrounding hullabaloo.
> —Sylvia Plath

"Depression is a luxury you can't afford." Ouch! An older gentleman actually said this to me! I was twenty-three years-old, trying to return to living after a rough and rapid descent into an alcoholic abyss. I was at a recovery clubhouse where 12-Step meetings of various types were held. We were in the cafeteria area after an AA meeting. I'm sure I looked at him with rancor. Who did he think he was? Did he think I wanted to be depressed? That I was choosing it? "Luxury"?

And then the old-timer continued, "Eventually, depression for you or me will deliver us back to drinking, and for us, as alcoholics, this is sure death. You can't afford it. When you awaken every morning, get down on your knees and say out loud, 'Thank You for this day'—I don't care what you do or do not believe in, just surrender." Surrender is an essential ingredient in the recipe for recovery.

Another essential and profound principle of recovery in 12-Step programs is to be of service to others in need who are beginning this recovery journey. This tenet also shows up in most religions and spiritual communities. There is a basic human yearning to help others by lending aid and support to those who are weakened, hurt, disabled, or unable. The simple act of reaching out to others changes everything; it transforms us, as it did for me. It allowed a metamorphosis of the implosion and depression I was experiencing.

In that same week at the Clubhouse, another "old-timer" (someone with decades of sobriety) asked me to go talk with a young woman around my age who was four days sober. I looked back at the old-timer with incredulity. She had craggy lines etched into her face, a past smoker, evident in her low gravelly voice.

I said, "I can't do that! I've only had a couple of weeks sober myself! I don't have anything to offer!"

This wizened old woman replied, "You are the closest to where she finds herself right now. She won't relate to me with twenty-five years of sobriety. Your story is the closest to hers. It will be the most powerful message for her to hear how you have made it ten more days than she has!"

And so, share with this young woman I did! After that day, many many more times when I could be of service, I offered. This simple act of service shifts the directional flow of energy from self-directed, stagnant, and self-absorbed to outer-directed, self-less and vital.

Back to the man's comment about not being able to afford the "luxury" of depression: His commentary turned my head. Okay, yes, it also pissed me off, but it definitely got my attention. Was depression a choice? What could I do differently? How did I wind up here? And what in the heck was I supposed to do now? I did follow his suggestion to surrender each morning by presenting a heart filled with gratitude, even when I had to fake it. I said it, "Thank You for this day."

As a physician, I've observed that depression is not a very precise diagnosis, and that a doctor's usual interest in it, beyond reaching for the prescription pad, is minimal. It's kind of a blanket term used to cover a great many states of being. And the etiologies for why the state exists is rarely scrutinized or diligently pursued in the usual medical circles.

There are multiple physiological states that can cause a person to feel depressed. Depression might stem from severe fatigue or chronic insomnia or continuous pain. We might feel a low mood from a hypo-functioning thyroid gland, imbalanced sex hormones (estrogen, progesterone, testosterone), neurotransmitter deficiencies (serotonin, dopamine, GABA, etc.), or a chronically stressed HPA system (adrenals). And then, additionally, there are all the mental/emotional elements that might converge and land an individual in a state of depression: a genetic predisposition, life events (tragedy, trauma, loss), and dysfunctional family dynamics. It's often layered and complex. (In rock-speak, it would be more like Vishnu schist than limestone!)

I was depressed again at age twenty-three. And now I can see, over forty years later, that it was somewhat like running into a familiar acquaintance with whom I'd lost touch. I'd known depression quite well at age thirteen. The shutting down, the giving up, the all-inclusive sense of resignation… like burrowing into a dark and quiet black hole… and sleeping and sleeping and sleeping. These hallmarks of my state of existence became habitual behaviors and feelings. And once something is "habitual," it is creating ruts in some of the brain's pathways. If you've ever driven a vehicle on a road with deep ruts in it, and then had the tires slide into these etched troughs, even in a four-wheel drive, you know it isn't easy to bump up out of those grooves. The vehicle wants to stay in these ruts (the path of least resistance). If you try to get out of them, your vehicle can even become high-centered in the furrows and get stuck. Disrupting this brain circuitry and neuro chemistry ingrained by the patterns of depression can be similarly challenging. It will usually require an emotional tow-truck and concerted effort to get un-stuck.

Despite the misery, despondency and dejection I was experiencing (both at thirteen or twenty-three years of age), there was also comfort, or at least a growing familiarity, with depression. It can seem like a safe and cozy, warm cocoon during a difficult or terrifying time. Something in me felt broken and I thought that whatever it was, it was unfixable and rendered me hopeless. Those who tried to help by saying perky things were more annoying than comforting. That's because you can't talk someone out of depression. It's an inside job.

Deciphering the root causes for disease, illness, conditions, and discomfort is essential. We need a formative context. And with depression,

I think it's especially critical to understand. It's why I'm an ND and not an MD as to doctoring careers. When I was nearing the completion of my bachelor's degree in pre-med, and planning for conventional medical school, I worked a night shift at a hospital, shadowing a physician to gain exposure to the field of medicine.

On this particular night, we had a "code blue" and we all raced to the room number announced over the intercom. This male patient was in cardiac arrest. He looked still and lifeless when we arrived. The team performed CPR, and then a few others got the defibrillator hooked up. "Clear" the doctor commanded! And like a TV episode in a medical series, it worked! The man's heartbeat returned. He was revived! He would live to see another day, even though mere moments before he had been passing on to the Other Side.

As I reflected about this later that night, I wondered about the man. What did he think about it all? Did he feel lucky, or did he feel scared? Did he wonder, "What caused this and how can it be prevented from happening again?" There seemed to be no follow-up or discussion about what had led up to his heart being overwrought and finally crying cardiac "uncle"! All of us—everyone who had shared that crisis moment—just returned to life as we knew it, including him. But this did not sit right with me. In fact, it seemed blatantly wrong. In addition to applying the life-saving efforts to save him when he was in acute distress and dying, why wouldn't we try to correct the causes and conditions that led to his heart attack?

So how should we begin to address depression? There are so many ways to intercede. The good news is that any way we start IS a way in, meaning that there is not just one right way to correct for depression.

In my experience, a Natural Medicine Practitioner works to address root causes, so that we can heal underlying issues that make us more prone to depression. If you visit an ND, for example, they might work to retrain and rebuild the adrenal system (HPA axis), and it will reach our mood. If we are newly diagnosed with hypothyroidism, and get appropriate treatment, it will reach our mood. If we find a solution to chronic pain and it lessens or is resolved, it will reach our mood. If we find an excellent therapist who helps us successfully address our past family of origin issues and trauma, it will reach our mood! It does not seem to matter what the portal is. The key is to alter the pattern! The key is to bump up out of the neural "ruts" (even momentarily). The key is to get in and lower the amount of imbalance and suffering on any level, and this will allow the whole being to recalibrate and re-balance.

The healing power of being seen and loved by someone is another potent portal into relieving depression. It only takes one person. In my case, it was my mother at age thirteen, and then, at twenty-three, it was an excellent, insightful and warm therapist. She held out a hand to help me get up again. She saw the creative genius (which we all possess) in me, and this helped me see it and believe it too. These individuals threw me a proverbial life preserver which facilitated my swim to emotional and spiritual safety. Their love, their presence and their unconditional witnessing of me—the real me—allowed me to piece together the puzzle of my fragmented self at those times and to recalibrate and reintegrate.

Depression is "a luxury I cannot afford," even as I face a terminal diagnosis. If you are reading this and you are depressed… go ahead—first, you can look at me (figuratively) with the same rancor and indignation I had for the old man who said it to me forty years ago—and then I hope you can see that this statement is not an indictment or judgment on the state you find yourself in, but rather an invitation: "Thank You for this day."

Truly: "There is no time not to live!"

Question #13:
How do you cope with chronic pain?

I will share some poignant thoughts as someone dealing with chronic pain. It causes great suffering for many people. For example, I received this question from someone who suffers chronic pain and debilitating disease: "I'm very aware that I tend to use victim language. What's the difference between taking responsibility for my life, especially my physical disease and pain, versus its being my fault? Is all this going on at an unconscious level as a pattern or habit of thought, or is it a lack of trust based upon early feelings of betrayal or abandonment?"

Physical illnesses and chronic pain pose a conundrum. It is incredibly tricky and complex to navigate. We need to accept the reality of our circumstances and also at the same time, not allow a diagnosis or chronic pain to become our central identity!

I am mindful not to become entwined and enmeshed with having illness or a terminal diagnosis. I do not say or think "my" cancer. I do not view myself as a cancer "victim." I make a conscious effort to speak in positive terms and without signaling my body and my Being that who we are is "ill," for this implies somehow broken, incomplete, or less than. We can inadvertently slip off into becoming a diagnosis. Soon, everything revolves around this, and everyone revolves around us with the diagnosis being the centrifugal force—front and center.

Louise Hay, author of books on self-healing, was onto something profound. And her premise was simply this: "Your body is always listening." Are you telling it, thinking, verbally stating, that you are a victim of illness or that you are "sickness"? Or are you telling your body that you are strong and able to find ways to experience joy and practice compassion, no matter what?

Labels trap us. Instead of "my cancer," I say "a diagnosis I've received." Or sometimes I do not name it all but rather I say, "Today I feel this way or that (I have a headache and some pain) and here's what would comfort me (a hot bath, a cup of tea, a movie, a pain med, etc.)."

We are so much more than our diagnoses, our pain, our symptoms at any given moment. And we are the only ones who can fight to preserve this—our personal agency.

I love my body for carrying me this far, and I promise my body that I'll do whatever I can to make things work and to make it as comfortable as possible—today. Just today. No global thinking or future awfulizing. Just taking tender loving care today.

Being loving toward myself and my body, no matter what, is an aspect of Wholeness, and it's an attitude many of us must re-learn. Somewhere along the way we may have practiced not paying attention to the body, ignoring its signals and treating our bodies poorly. And soon we've become entirely disconnected from the physical self and all its communications. Our first job is to get back in touch, deeply present with our wondrous physical aspect. On a given day—upon deciding to be in bed most of the day, for example—I work to have no shame, no apology. I am not weak. I am not defective. I have not done anything wrong to wind up here. Instead, I am listening closely to what IS, paying attention to the present, just as it is.

I have been through periods of incredible pain with the multiple myeloma diagnosis I've been given. Sometimes the pain is at a 10 out of 10 on that scale of 1 to 10, with 10 being the worst. When relapsing, I am slowed to nearly a standstill. This is a dramatic shift from times of remission and better health which are filled with activity, such as hiking, some biking and a bit of rowing. I love to cook, gather with a friend and have deep dive discussions about the meaning of life! I dabble in the creative arts with writing and painting. I have a meditation practice that is very important to me. But this can all fall away and be gone in a seeming flash, and then I am experiencing disease again.

Pain and illness zap inspiration and enthusiasm. It usually lands me on that island of isolation. It is quite depressing, and one could easily slip off into an abyss of despondency when in its grips. But I have found that acknowledging all these attendant feelings, getting really present to what is happening right now, then also remembering that I am so much more than this moment of pain. It helps. It's the opening to Acceptance and Surrender.

I say to myself: "Okay, this is what IS right now. And it's okay. Dear body, I love you for working so hard for me, trying with all your fortitude and might to help me. You are an amazing and incredible warrior. Just rest and know you are beautiful and everything is okay, even with all that you are experiencing right now."

The presence of someone I love is deeply comforting. I may not want to talk or interact much, but I love feeling their presence. I like someone reading or working on something just near me. I think the presence of another beating heart is a profound medicine and should not be underestimated. It is also why my sweet Australian Shepherd, Jenga, delivers such deep and beautiful comfort during difficult times.

We are not alone but, yes, it is still a solo flight. There it is, I think. We do not want to be alone and especially when we are suffering and in pain. It is changed by the presence of another. It is profoundly transformed by Love in the room with us.

I learned some years ago as I sat with a dear friend in Hospice, that there was less and less to say. Even though we didn't talk, the room never felt empty as I sat with her. I could feel her Presence despite her weaving in and out of consciousness. It was big. I learned to show up. It felt hard not to "do" something, but I gradually learned that this quiet room, inhabited by her and me, was filled with Us. All the years of our friendship, all of our accumulated moments of tears together and our great many times of nearly-peeing-our-pants laughter together, our intimate confiding, our proverbial rescue of each other (emotionally running to the other for shelter when life's crises hit), sitting with her for these many hospice hours taught me that there was meaning held within this togetherness in the silence.

Someone once told me that they learned to be helpless in order to try to get others to care for them. Whoa! "Learned helplessness." This is complicated and set in motion by unmet childhood needs. So yes, we must look at reenactment. We must do our work and become conscious of all of it. The impact of betrayal and abandonment from childhood doesn't just damage us at the time or disappear upon reaching adulthood, but this assault on our precious psyches leaves a blueprint for all future relationships. We proceed through life unconsciously trying to stop the bleeding, to mend the hurting. We may still carry a child's birthright and innate longing to be cherished and perfectly loved.

We cannot remain in this closed circuit of reenactment and find any semblance of Wholeness. We can break free and become conscious and aware so that we will not need to reenact and repeat old patterns anymore! Sometimes we play the victim because this is how we learned (as children) to treat ourselves. Sometimes, it was the only tenderness we could find. On one hand, it's kind of a lovely thing—our seeking to bring focus and aid through self-pity. Yet, on the other hand, it's a long-ago outgrown thing. We are adults now. We have agency. We can and must do better. We get to decide. Some say that we teach others how to treat us. Helpless or empowered? Weak or strong? Open or closed? Conscious and awake, or unaware and asleep? We get to decide.

No one else can assign meaning or metaphor to our health-related conditions. Only we, individually, can find the Path forward when struck with physical impediments, ailments and disease. All of one's life is the fodder for making meaning, grist for the awakening mill, and each of us is responsible for whether or not we accept this challenge when presented with chronic Illness.

Obviously, I did not hope to have a terminal diagnosis, and I did not do something wrong to inadvertently bring this upon myself. I did not unconsciously hope to die of the exact same cancer that took my mother's life four months after her diagnosis. But I can look with open eyes and an open heart to the meaning that may lay hidden in the dark crevices of my mind. I can explore my own patterns of deep codependence with her and her moods. I can consider my childlike wishes to take all of my mother's pain from her (when growing up).

With a conscious eye, I can flush all of this out from under the dense thicket of my psyche. I can choose to change my story's ending by learning and listening as the layers that had remained obscured or hidden are peeled back. It releases me to raise these past wounds to consciousness. Learning how to grieve has been a critical part of my healing—whether old layers of loss are being uncovered or it is a new and current hurt—grieving (feeling feelings) is the way through. I can experience freedom and wonder on any given day, even on those days when I must rest and be still.

Question #14:
How does it feel to be you right this moment?

Fantastic and crummy! The old mixed bag.

Yesterday, my husband and I were driving on Hwy 101. We were on our way to a small port town while vacationing along the Oregon Coast. We didn't make it to our destination. We got caught in a major traffic jam, eight miles long, due to a fatal motor vehicle accident up ahead. While sitting there in our now stopped car—hearing there were possibly numerous casualties and Life Flight helicopters on their way—the severity of the crash settled over me.

I thought, *Wow, here these people were, on an early Monday morning, just driving to work or continuing their sightseeing or doing some ordinary errand, and nothing they did that morning before getting into their cars had allowed for this!* They didn't have a chance to bring closure or completeness to their endings. Nothing in them imagined that their death was even possible in the next hour. Maybe they were focused on getting a good cup of coffee! There would be no tidying up, no getting affairs in order, no last words, no good-byes for them. In an instant—they were gone from our world.

And then, I was trying to reconcile this accident with my life, right here, right now, in this moment. Here I am, still here, waiting in our now turned-off car, contending with a terminal illness diagnosis, yet very much alive! We just don't get to know. On this morning, my experience of this occurrence resets me. I—and everyone else out here in this traffic jam—we just don't get to know how long we'll be here.

Currently, I am suspended between hope and despair because I am relapsing again. It's been a roller coaster for almost eight years now. Whenever disease returns to my body, I recognize that when I'm in remission and my body feels better, it all seems more like a dream—until it's not—and suddenly it is real again. So very real. When illness returns, my mind races (fear), my heart aches (sad), and my body talks (pain).

I deeply desire meaning in life, and I want to contribute more meaning in others' experiences if I can. Finding purpose is one way we generate meaning. So far, in many ways, I have had a fantastic life, rich with experiences that created the fertile soil for growing my True Self and cultivating Purpose. They say the warrior's path (which we are all on, if we choose it) is strengthened by learning how to show up, no matter what, just as we are, and then staying—no matter what!

We all want to be comfortable, yet we are most alive when we are challenged. (Not too challenged, as in traumatized, but pushed enough to feel our edges.) Last week, I hit my edges when I tried to go through a box of old stuff (memorabilia and saved items). Sounds benign, I know. This stuff had been neatly tucked away and stored out of sight for years and even decades. But for some reason, this week, I pulled it out from storage to shed some daylight on its contents and additionally accomplish the ambitious goal to clear out this closet.

However, one cardboard box, stuffed with junior high and high school saved items, had the power to practically topple me over. I felt crummy and exhausted after looking through it. Feeling bad in this diffuse way was disconcerting. I decided today was not the day for this. Back to the closet the box was returned. But I did wonder: Is it lost memory, is it a traumatic whisper from my past, or is it just a dust allergy?!

I didn't have a horrendous childhood—on the surface of things. Yet I have sustained injury nearly the same as if I had. The damage to my person was more like the smoldering, slow-burn type of trauma or what a friend of mine calls, "death by 1,000 papercuts." This childhood trauma was inflicted quietly, innocuously, yet frequently.

I think I worked hard to forget, and then after that, I also worked really hard to remember (through therapy, 12-Step work, spiritual dedication). So why am I sometimes still frozen and disabled by "it" when being reminded of certain eras from the past? And what is "it"?

I ask truly and deeply: What is "it" that I don't yet understand, don't have a path back to, or don't want to look at?

I think adolescence is our first big walking-across-hot-coals-barefooted exercise in life. It is an extremely intense and challenging time for all who enter. It begins when our bodies change from that of a child's shape to adult form, and then continues with all the insecurities, confusion, and confounding socialization.

One evening, I was in the kitchen, getting ready to leave for a football game where my 9th grade band would be playing. My dad had entered the room and briefly stood watching me. I was dressed in jeans and a snug, navy blue turtleneck sweater. I was standing with my coat draped over my arm, and peering out the window above the sink, waiting for my ride. My dad approached closer, and in a sudden motion, flicked my C-cup breast from underneath and upward with his forefinger and asked me angrily (like a low shout): "What do you have in there?" His rage was palpable. I was stunned and horrified. Embarrassment crept up my neck to my face with a red-hot flush. I answered, "Nothing!!" I stood motionless, holding my breath and staring down into the stainless steel sink until he left the room. I waited for my breathing to slow and my heartbeat to quiet, still clutching the edge of the Formica countertop.

My ride appeared and I pulled on my jacket and went to the game. I'm sure I sat where the music was emanating from the rest of the pep band. I can guess that I played my rhythm-keeping French horn parts well enough. I probably cheered for our team. I likely chatted with my bandmates throughout the game. Maybe I got concessions at halftime. I imagine I appeared "fine" to everyone around me. However, I don't remember a single minute or even a split second of that game.

In addition to the physical transformation, being a teenager goes down an intricate and confusing social path. Suddenly, it's as if all the rules of engagement have been changed. And I remember feeling like I was the only one who didn't get the handbook. Little did I know then that everyone was scrambling to find a social foothold, everyone was trying to brace themselves against embarrassment, criticism, humiliation, invisibility, and friendlessness. We all sought and longed for some sense of security. But mistakenly, I assumed I was a misfit, like an ugly stranger in a new and beautiful land.

I recall an exercise that I did from a self-help book while in my thirties (over thirty years ago). It said to stand in front of the mirror, and while gazing at yourself, say the words: "I Love Myself Unconditionally" and you repeat this phrase, twenty or more times. Whoa! At first, this was difficult—nearly impossible—for me. It triggered my resistance and caused me pain. A heavy and sad feeling of old grief filled me. Tears sprang forth before I knew what was happening. Voices inside said, "No, we don't love you unconditionally." The tears were old and buried somewhere back there with puberty, adolescence and before. Now here they flowed. The simple exercise elicited feelings that I couldn't simplify or ignore.

Present-day, the contents of the box of old stuff were now triggering some phases of my earlier life, rustling up some past selves who were still waiting for me to retrieve and integrate them. These parts were going to need a lot of loving. Good news for me: I had gained the skills to do that. The box can wait until I'm ready to go through it.

(A few weeks later). I went after that box today. Entering it, I felt my wholeness and was ready to feel what I would feel and support the parts of me that had been abandoned back then. Even by telling the narrative above, I was able to get in touch with lost and dissociated aspects of myself.

This has been, in my life, an ongoing process of inner work. I have both had to find a way back to my original feelings (like that evening before the football game), feel them while loving every inch of myself, and emotionally hold my dad accountable for the harms done.

Once aware I can then shed daylight, love, and complete acceptance on these lost selves. Today I feel profound sympathy for the girl I had been. I feel deep compassion for the young woman I was becoming back then. And I continue to acknowledge and process how harmful my dad's reactivity to my development was for me. Next follows a beautiful freedom!

Tree by the road.

Epilogue
Dear Reader, I Hope You Know This…

Sometimes, it can be so damn hard to be here… but know that you and I are in it together, whether we've never met or have known each other forever. You are just like me, and I am just like you. It takes fierceness and commitment to stay in this Ring of Life, fighting. I know it. You know it. By sharing some of the most difficult moments from my life, I am wanting to say to you:

"You can do it!"

"You can rise to this challenge."

"You can dare to stay a little bit longer and you can make meaning of this too."

"Step solidly toward becoming more of who you are meant to be by showing up right now, for yourself."

Here in this interview is some of what it has taken to soften me, to smooth some of my rough edges, to open me, and allow me finally to dare to be Fully Alive.

What are you waiting for?

About the Author

Erin Lommen, ND, worked as a Naturopathic Doctor in family medicine for over thirty years. Career highlights include the pioneering of neuroendocrine solutions for addictions, and a successful five-year study through the NIH (National Institute of Health) on chronic disease. Dr. Lommen taught as an associate professor at NCNM (National College of Naturopathic Medicine) for ten years and is the co-author of the popular book, *Slim, Sane and Sexy: Pocket Guide to Natural, Bioidentical Hormone Balancing*. She was a sought-after presenter at national and international conferences on a multitude of health topics, as well as television interviews locally and nationally (e.g., CNN).

After a terminal diagnosis and a life-altering dream (described in this book), Erin left private practice as a physician and brought her public speaking career to a close. Her focus turned inward, to the True Self. She became committed to more open-heartedness and vulnerability in her relationships. She went more deeply into her spiritual journey. A lifelong nature lover, Erin enjoyed hiking in the woods with her beloved dog, Jenga, and volunteering to feed lions at the Lion Habitat Ranch in Nevada. She was grateful for her husband and two children and the experience of Love she was privileged to have with them. People who knew Erin describe her as a pioneering physician, loving friend, and a wise, authentic, deep soul.

In the last months of her life, Erin found meaning in offering her most honest inner Self in a dialogue on death with two other women. One was Karen Derris, a Buddhist scholar-professor with terminal brain cancer. The other was Caroline McGuigan, a psychotherapist in Ireland whose husband was brutally murdered and died in her arms. These powerful dialogues were recorded for the public.

About the Interviewer

Fran Grace, PhD, is Emerita (retired) Professor of Religious Studies at the University of Redlands, where she pioneered a contemplative approach to university education for twenty-five years. Academic life, however, did not fulfill her deep inner quest for truth. In 2003, a life crisis broke open her inner world, and she encountered her teacher, Dr. David R. Hawkins, who taught her the "inner pathway" that respects the essence of all spiritual traditions. She moved to live near him and spent many years working closely with him. The impact was life-changing. In 2008, by his directive, she created Inner Pathway (The Institute for Contemplative Life), a 501c3 nonprofit organization dedicated to the "inner pathway." Before her teacher's death in 2012, she edited and wrote the forewords to his widely popular books *Letting Go: The Pathway of Surrender* and the official revision of his *Power vs. Force*. Her book, *The Power of Love*, is a Silver Award winner in the Benjamin Franklin Book Awards for "Best Inspirational Books in 2019." Following the sudden death of her partner's son, she was certified as a death doula to serve the dying and their loved ones.

About the Publisher

Inner Pathway Publishing is the trade name for the Institute for Contemplative Life, a 501(c)(3) nonprofit organization created by Dr. Fran Grace in 2008, as directed by her teacher. Our purpose is to support the "inner pathway" of all who come to us. We do this by offering unique books, workshops, retreats, films, and classes that come from verified spiritual teachings. The inner pathway is timeless and open to all, free of dogma, dues, or membership. Therefore, our offerings are nondogmatic and nonpromotional. They exist simply to inspire the inner qualities of compassion, wisdom, love, joy, beauty, humor, and truth in a way that is of practical benefit in the present world.

Contact Information:
www.innerpathway.com
info@innerpathway.com

PO Box 1435
Redlands, California
92373 USA

Additional Titles:
The Power of Love: A Transformed Heart Changes the World
by Fran Grace

I Give You the Springtime of My Blushing Heart: A Poetic Love Song
by Dedan Gills and Belvie Rooks

Love is Forever
by Fran Grace